LAND ROVER

Series I, II, III & V8

LAND-ROVER
JWK 772N

LAND-ROVER

Series I, II, III & V8

◆

ESSENTIAL
ADVICE & DATA
FOR
BUYERS & ENTHUSIASTS

◆

James Taylor

Windrow & Greene Automotive

Published in Great Britain by
Windrow & Greene Ltd
5 Gerrard Street
London W1V 7LJ

A CIP catalogue record for this book is available from the British Library.

ISBN 1 872004 12 1

Design: *ghk* DESIGN, Chiswick, London

Printed by Craft Print (Europe) Ltd.

Contents

INTRODUCTION AND ACKNOWLEDGEMENTS

Land-Rovers come in all shapes and sizes, and to cover all of them would have taken many more pages than were made available to me. One of the hardest parts of writing this book was therefore deciding what to leave out. In the end, I decided to concentrate on the most numerous Land-Rovers — the leaf-sprung, normal-control models built between 1948 and 1985.

Even within that framework, the number of different models is enormous. But I hope that the advice contained in this book covers enough of their common points to prevent readers from making expensive mistakes when buying an older Land-Rover, be it for fun or for business.

Lots of people helped with pictures to illustrate the points I needed to make. My thanks go to Roger Crathorne and Paul O'Connor at Land Rover Ltd, to Mike Thom and Ken Band at Land Rover Parts, to Richard Thomas at *Land Rover Owner* magazine, to Mike Pullinger at Brooklyn Engineering, to Mark Griffiths at the Land Rover Centre in Huddersfield, and to Brian Bashall, John Craddock, Peter Hobson and Guy Pickford.

Note: *to anyone confused by the now-you-see-it-now-you don't hyphen in Land-Rover: the name was always hyphenated for its first 30 years. The hyphen was first omitted in 1978 when Land Rover Ltd was established, but remained in general use until the beginning of the 1980s. To avoid confusion, this book hyphenates the name when referring to the vehicles, but omits the hyphen in references to the company and its present offshoots.*

James Taylor
Woodcote, Reading, December 1992

The Author

James Taylor first began researching automotive history as a part-time activity in the late 1970s and has developed wide interests in both classic and modern cars. Now a full-time motoring journalist, he writes regularly for leading British motoring magazines and for several overseas publications. Among the many books he has written on a variety of marques are *The Land-Rover 1948-1988* and *Classics In Colour: Land Rover*.

1. Origins of the Land-Rover

During the lifetime of the Land-Rover, a most extraordinary change in customer perception of its role has taken place. Originally conceived as a multi-purpose workhorse for agricultural and light industrial use, it has become an enthusiast's vehicle *par excellence*.

The reasons are not difficult to identify. The original Land-Rover proved itself so reliable and so durable in adverse conditions that it inspired fierce devotion in many of its owners. Its remarkable ability to clamber across rough terrain and through axle-deep mud also made owners wonder whether there was any terrain difficult enough to defeat it, and in due course it became something of a challenge to find such terrain. Out of that developed the off-road sports which are today a major feature of the Land-Rover enthusiasts' world. But perhaps most important of all is that the Land-Rover is one of the very few vehicles which can be taken apart and put back together again by an amateur, using only basic tools. Designed to be simple to repair in the outback or the bush, it is also simple to work on at home.

So what lies behind this charismatic vehicle? Who thought up the original concept, which has proved so durable that today's Land-Rovers are instantly recognisable as the descendants of the original vehicles of nearly 45 years ago? To answer that question, we must first take a look at the difficult conditions facing the British motor industry as it emerged from the 1939-1945 War with Hitler's Germany.

The War had left the British economy in tatters. There was massive overseas debt, and the primary task of the Government was to get Britain out of the red. To that end, it set about persuading British manufacturers to earn foreign currency by concentrating on selling their products overseas. As far as the motor industry was concerned, it set targets: 50% of annual production was to be exported in 1945; 60% and later 70% in 1947; and 75% by 1949.

The Government also had a potent weapon to ensure that manufacturers adhered to this policy. The dislocation of the War had caused supplies of raw materials to be at best erratic and at worst non-existent, and so a new Ministry of Supply was established to deal with the problems. That Ministry took on the responsibility for all raw materials supplies, with the effect that it could not only provide supplies but could also cut them off. To help enforce its export quota requirements, the Government arranged for the Ministry of Supply to cut off supplies of sheet steel from motor manufacturers who failed to comply.

The Rover Company found itself in a difficult position within all this. It had never taken export markets at all seriously before the War, deigning only to supply cars to the British Colonies and then differentiating them from the home product only through the fitment of larger tyres. As the War drew to a close, it began planning for limited production of its pre-War models alongside a new small car which, the Directors reasoned, would have more appeal in the expected straitened economic climate than would the expensive, middle-class cars with which it had been associated in the 1930s. But when peace came, it soon became clear that overseas markets did not want this sort of car at all, and so the project was abandoned.

The newly-formed Export Department at Rover did its best with the company's medium-sized, middle-class cars, but overseas sales were slow.

The Rover Directors were desperate. To develop a new car with export appeal would take several years, and in the meantime Rover would somehow have to struggle along. The company needed a new product, and fast. Board Meeting minutes of the time show that the Directors' thoughts soon focussed on one new product proposal. This was an all-purpose vehicle on the lines of the Jeep, which had been dreamed up by Rover's Chief Engineer, Maurice Wilks. The Board was asked to approve it for production in September 1947, and Rover's development engineers completed the first prototype a month later.

A utility vehicle of this kind was a long way from the kind of urbane, middle-class cars that Rover had been producing, so why did it seem such an attractive option? There were three main reasons. First, there was a waiting market. The War had brought mechanisation for the first time to many undeveloped countries, and now that peace had been restored these same countries were clamouring for more mechanisation to help them in their agricultural and industrial development. They did not want cars: what they wanted were trucks, tractors and other utility vehicles. A particular favourite was the wartime Willys Jeep, left behind in its thousands by the Allied Forces and an ideal vehicle for work in countries where proper roads were non-existent. The second reason why the utility vehicle appealed to the Rover Directors was that it would be quick, easy and cheap to put into production. As a utility vehicle did not need the aesthetic appeal of a car, it could have very simple body panelling which could be made up by hand. That would save on both the time and the expense of having new press-tools made up. With a little ingenuity, it would also be possible to adapt a number of existing major Rover car components to suit such a vehicle, thus again saving time and money. And thirdly, it should be possible to get adequate supplies of the raw materials needed to build it. The body panels could be of readily- available aircraft aluminium alloy. As for the rationed steel content, if Rover could get their new vehicle classified as a commercial vehicle rather than as a passenger car, it would automatically get preferential treatment from the Ministry of Supply.

Rover's first prototype, built up in October 1947, was actually built on the chassis of a War-surplus Jeep, and also used a number of its running components. With its original 1.3-litre Rover engine and a central steering position designed to save the cost of making separate left-hand- and right-hand-drive versions, it had a number of flaws; but the Rover development engineers could see that it had tremendous potential. So it was that the Rover Board sanctioned the new vehicle for production in September 1947. A pre-production batch of 48 ironed out the last remaining problems, and production began in earnest in July 1948, after pre-production cars had been displayed at the Amsterdam Motor Show in April. Rover called its new vehicle the Land-Rover.

The wartime Willys Jeep was the inspiration behind Rover's decision to produce a utility vehicle for Britain's export markets, many of them newly mechanised.

Below: The first Land-Rover prototype was built in 1947 and borrowed its central steering position from agricultural tractor practice.

Overleaf
Main picture: The 48 pre-production vehicles built in the early part of 1948 were very similar to the eventual production Land-Rover. The indicator lamps under the bumper of this restored example are a later addition.
Insert: Solihull, home of the Land-Rover. It had begun life as a 'shadow' factory for Britain's military aircraft industry in the 1930s. This picture shows the site much as it is today: there were far fewer buildings on the site when the Land-Rover went into production in 1948.

2. Production history

As its title makes clear, this book deals only with the normal-control Land-Rovers and not with the much rarer Forward Control models. It also confines itself to the leaf-sprung models, which went out of production in 1985. The coil-sprung Land-Rovers — introduced in 1983 and thus overlapping with the final years of leaf-sprung Land-Rover production — are not considered.

Incredible as it may seem, the Land-Rover remained fundamentally unchanged between its introduction in 1948 and the demise of the leaf-sprung models in 1985. Certainly, it grew larger, gained more powerful engines, and became (slightly) more refined. But throughout those 37 years, it retained its original simple design. All the Land-Rovers under consideration here had box-section steel chassis with beam axles and semi-elliptic leaf springs; they all had bolt-on bodies with corrosion-resistant alloy panels; and the very last Series III was immediately recognisable as the lineal descendant of the 1948 80-inch.

Series I models

No Land-Rover was ever called a Series I until the Series II models were announced in 1958, so the description is a retrospective one. Nevertheless, the Rover Company regularly used the term Series I after 1958 and it gained currency.

The first Land-Rovers had an 80-inch wheelbase and were powered by a 1595cc IOE four-cylinder petrol engine. They came as spartan soft-top or open models, although an optional hard top with cab roof was introduced in 1950 and a coachbuilt seven-seater Station Wagon was available between October 1948 and mid-1951.

The first 1500 Land-Rovers had a freewheel in the drivetrain to counteract axle wind-up in the permanent four-wheel-drive system, but this was discontinued in October 1950 in favour of a selectable 2WD/4WD system. Vehicles built before May 1950 had their headlamps concealed behind the wire mesh grille, but after that date the headlamps were exposed.

More road performance arrived in mid-1951 when a 2-litre engine was substituted for the earlier type. However, the re-engined 80-inch model lasted in production only two years. Customers were demanding more and more carrying capacity, and so in autumn 1953, two new and larger Land-Rovers replaced the 80-inch type.

The new models both had longer wheelbases and longer load beds to match. The direct replacement for the 80-inch model had an 86-inch wheelbase and an increased rear overhang, which together gave nine more inches in the load bed. The new long-wheelbase model had 107 inches between the axle centres and a full six feet of length in its load bed. From mid-1954, a seven-seater Station Wagon was offered on the 86-inch chassis and, during 1956, a 10-seater model was made available on the 107-inch chassis.

There were detail modifications over the next two years, as indeed there always would be throughout the Land-Rover's production life. The next major change, however, came in the autumn of 1956, when the wheelbases of both models were stretched by two inches. The 86-inch thus became

Above: The dumpy look of the original 80-inch Land-Rover is clearly apparent in this picture of a 1950 example.
Below: One of the few failures in Land-Rover history was the 80-inch Station Wagon.

an 88-inch and the 107-inch became a 109-inch.

This time, the wheelbase stretch was not used to make the load-bed larger, but to allow extra room in the engine bay. The new engine around which the Land-Rovers had been redesigned did not actually become available until June 1957, however. It was a 2-litre OHV four-cylinder diesel, introduced after repeated requests from customers, and was the first compression-ignition engine Rover had ever made. Though crude and noisy, it was effective in meeting a long-standing need. Petrol and diesel 88-inch and 107-inch models continued side by side until April 1958, when a completely revised Land-Rover range was introduced.

Series II models

The Series II Land-Rovers were characterised by two major innovations. On the mechanical side, they had a new and more powerful 2.25-litre OHV petrol engine in place of the 2-litre IOE type. This new engine had been developed in tandem with the 2-litre diesel engine, which remained available, and the two engines had many design features in common. The second major innovation was that the Series II Land-Rovers had benefited from the attentions of the Rover Styling Department. While they were still recognisably Land-Rovers and still appropriately rugged-looking, they were much neater in appearance than the Series Is had been. Most important among the changes were slightly wider bodies below the window-line, with a curved 'step' which gave new character to the slab-sides, and sill panels hiding the exhaust and fuel tank, which had been only too visible on the Series Is.

The basic body options remained as before — although the truck cab had been neatly restyled as part of the overall facelift — but there would be no Series II long-wheelbase Station Wagon until autumn 1958. In the meantime, the Series I 107-inch Station Wagon stood in. The Series II 88-inch and 109-inch models, with petrol or diesel options, then continued in production until the summer of 1961.

Series IIA models

The Series IIA was little more than a refinement of the Series II. The only major change was to the diesel engine, which now came as a 2.25-litre and shared the bore and stroke dimensions of the petrol alternative. The extra 11bhp and 15 lbs/ft of torque which this capacity increase brought were very welcome, but the Rover designers had also paid

LAND-ROVER PRODUCTION CHRONOLOGY

(NORMAL CONTROL, LEAF-SPRUNG MODELS)

1948 (April)	Land-Rover announced at Amsterdam Show.
1951 (August)	2-litre engine replaces 1.6-litre.
1953 (September)	86-inch model replaces 80-inch; 107-inch introduced.
1956 (September)	88-inch and 109-inch models replace 86-inch and 107-inch; 107-inch Station Wagon remains in production.
1957 (June)	2-litre diesel engine introduced; not available in 107-inch Station Wagon.
1958 (April)	Series II Land-Rovers introduced, with 88-inch and 109-inch wheelbases. 2.25-litre petrol engine replaces 2-litre.
1958 (September)	109-inch Station Wagon replaces 107-inch.
1959 (November)	250,000th Land-Rover built.
1961 (September)	Series IIA Land-Rovers introduced; 2.25-litre diesel engine replaces 2-litre.
1966 (April)	500,000th Land-Rover built.
1967 (April)	Six-cylinder petrol engine option introduced for 109-inch models.
1967 (September)	One-Ton model introduced.
1971 (June)	750,000th Land-Rover built.
1971 (September)	Series III Land-Rovers introduced.
1976 (June)	Millionth Land-Rover built.
1979 (February)	V8 petrol engine available in 109-inch models.
1981 (September)	2.25-litre petrol and diesel engines re-engineered with five main bearings instead of three.
1982 (April)	County Station Wagons introduced on 88-inch and 109-inch chassis; High Capacity Pick-Up introduced on 109-inch.
1983 (March)	New coil-sprung Land-Rover One Ten introduced to replace 109-inch Series III.
1984 (June)	New coil-sprung Land-Rover Ninety introduced to replace 88-inch Series III.
1985	Last leaf-sprung Land-Rovers built.

Above: Early Land-Rovers had the IOE engine. This is a 1.6-litre type; the later 2-litres looked broadly similar.

Left: The dashboard of the early Series I was very basic indeed. On this 1948 model, note the ring-pull control for the freewheel, in the floor beside the transfer box lever.

Below: The 86-inch model was intended to give increased loadspace. The extra length is clearly visible ahead of the rear wheel arch.

careful attention to noise levels, and the characteristic diesel clatter was considerably reduced on the larger engine.

In early 1962, 109-inch Station Wagons were reclassified as 12-seaters (and appropriate changes were made to the rear longitudinal seats) in order to avoid Purchase Tax. Overseas, however, where Purchase Tax did not apply, they remained 10-seaters. Otherwise, there were only small changes for the next five years, not least because the Land-Rover production lines were kept going at full stretch just to keep pace with orders. When spare cash did become available, therefore, the priority was always to increase production levels rather than to modify an already successful product. However, by adapting a redundant saloon car engine, the Rover engineers were able to provide Land-Rovers with more power from mid-1967.

The redundant saloon car engine (which had already appeared in export versions of the Forward Control Land-Rover based on the 109-inch chassis) was a 2.6-litre six-cylinder, belonging to the same IOE family as the early 1.6-litre and 2-litre Land Rover engines. It was offered only in the 109-inch wheelbase chassis, and there it had two main purposes. Firstly, it gave the Station Wagon more refined performance and a higher road speed, both of which Rover considered suitable for a passenger-carrying vehicle; and secondly, it allowed a new high-payload model to be introduced. This was known as the One-Ton Land Rover, and was essentially a beefed-up 109-inch model with stronger axles, larger tyres, and gearing changes.

A further important new model was introduced in 1968. This was the military Half-Ton, built on the 88-inch wheelbase and available only to military authorities. The original impetus for the design had come from the British Army, which wanted a Land-Rover light enough to be transported under the helicopters it then had in service. The Military Lightweight (to use its more familiar description) was therefore designed to have body panels which could be quickly removed and left behind when the vehicle was to be transported by helicopter. Those panels were also of very simple construction, without any of the styling in the civilian Series IIA's panels, and gave the Military Lightweight a uniquely stark appearance.

Series III models

The Series IIA models were replaced in September 1971 by the new Series III models. As before, these came with either an 88-inch or a 109-inch wheelbase, with 2.25-litre petrol or diesel engines (or the 2.6-litre six-cylinder petrol engine in 109-inch and One Ton models). The military lightweight on the 88-inch chassis remained a Series IIA until outstanding orders were completed during 1972, but all subsequent examples were to Series III specification. In all cases, the body variants remained as before.

Under the skin, Series III models benefited from a revised gearbox which now had synchromesh on all forward speeds. The heavy-duty clutch formerly fitted only to diesel and six-cylinder petrol models was standardised, and 109-inch models gained tougher half-shafts and a stronger rear axle. Brakes were improved by means of new drums with increased resistance to fade, and servo assistance became standard on all Station Wagons and six-cylinder models, and optional on other 109-inch variants. On the electrical side, welcome improvements included a repositioned battery, now under the bonnet instead of under the front seat, with an alternator instead of a dynamo.

Although Series III versions of the military lightweight were quite hard to distinguish from their Series IIA predecessors, other Series III Land-Rovers were very easy to recognise. Their main distinguishing feature was an injection-moulded ABS radiator grille instead of the earlier wire type. Windscreen and doors also had flatter hinges than before, and the nearside front wing now sported an air intake for the heater. There was also a completely revised interior, with instruments directly ahead of the driver for the first time, relocated switches with a stalk control for indicators, horn, headlamp flash and dipswitch, and padded crash-rails on the facia.

There were no more changes of note until 1974, when an overdrive (made by Fairey Winches) became available as an optional extra for the Land Rover, mainly in response to concern about fuel price increases after the 1973 Arab-Israeli War. No further changes would be made until 1979, because the financial troubles of the British Leyland conglomerate (which had bought out the Rover Company in 1967) prevented investment in new vehicles.

However, in 1978, the Land-Rover business was separated from the car-producing side of British Leyland, and a new subsidiary called Land Rover Ltd was established. This was granted £280 million for investment in expanded production and new models and, as far as the Series III Land-Rover was concerned, the first effects became apparent in 1979.

The 3.5-litre V8 engine which Rover had bought from General Motors in 1964 had been introduced to Rover saloon cars in 1967, and it was no surprise to find this (at last) in a Land-Rover. From February 1979, the Land-Rover V8 replaced the six-cylinder long-wheelbase Land-Rover, although there would be no V8s for the home market until the following year, and there would never be any 88-inch V8 models. The One-Ton Land-Rover ceased production at the same time as the new V8 109-inch appeared.

The Land-Rover V8 was essentially a Series III vehicle, but it was instantly recognisable by its flush-front with a new black plastic grille and, less subtly, by the 'Land Rover V8' decals on its rear flanks and the 'V8' decal at the back. The new model was also known as a 'Stage I' V8, both because there would be later V8 Land Rovers and because this one was produced under Stage I of the company's £280 million investment scheme.

The V8 engine was heavily detuned from its saloon-car application — and even from its Range Rover application — mainly because the existing drum brakes were simply not up to stopping a fully-laden 109-inch Land-Rover from speeds much higher than it could already reach. Nevertheless, the V8 offered both more power and more torque than the superseded six-cylinder engine, and the Land-Rover V8 was capable of higher cruising speeds. To avoid undue strain on the axles, selectable four-wheel drive had been replaced by a permanent four-wheel-drive system (where the torque is always evenly split between axles and cannot all be transmitted through a single axle as happens in two-wheel drive).

The final changes to Series III Land-Rovers came in April 1982, and belonged to Stage II of the company's investment scheme. Their main purpose was to combat increased competition from foreign 4x4 manufacturers (notably from Japan). In essence, they consisted of an alternative high-capacity pick-up body for the 109-inch models and of a De Luxe trim package which could be fitted to any Land-Rover model but would be specifically associated with the two Station Wagon models. The High-Capacity Pick-Up was more commonly known by its initials of HCPU and carried the same 1 tonne payload as the standard vehicle; but it was also available with uprated suspension to handle a 1.3-tonne payload. The De Luxe trim package turned standard 88-inch and 109-inch Station Wagons into County Station Wagons, and brought with it side stripes, 'County' decals, radial tyres, cloth trim and inertia-reel front safety belts. The 109-inch models were superseded in March 1983 by the new coil-sprung One Ten Land-Rovers, and the 88-inch

Right: The 107-inch Land-Rover was a companion to the 86-inch, again intended to offer more carrying capacity.

Below: The 107-inch Station Wagon was built up from existing body panels as far as was possible — hence its patchwork-quilt appearance.

Right: Demand from customers led to the introduction of the 2-litre diesel engine in 1957.

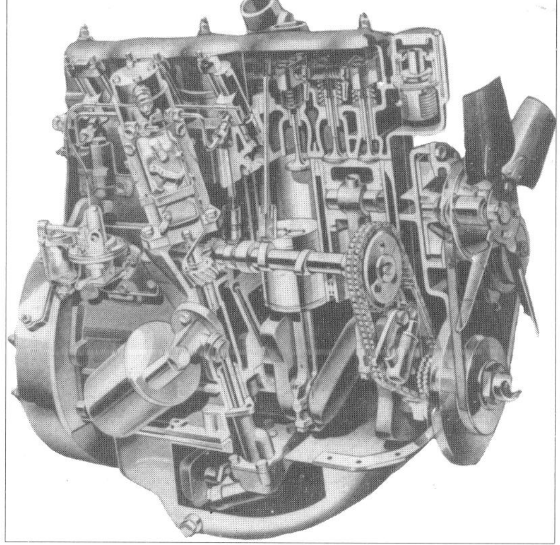

models were superseded in June 1984 by the Ninety models. However, actual production of the 109-inch models continued into 1985 to meet demand from export markets where fleet owners were initially reluctant to change to the very different One Ten.

Above: Most successful of the Series II styling revisions was the long-wheelbase Station Wagon. Compare this with the 107-inch Series I model! The example pictured is actually a Series IIA, dating from 1969.

Top: Series II models had a new 2¼-litre OHV petrol engine, which shared its principal design characteristics with the diesel engine. This is a later example, as fitted to Series III models in the 1970s.

Left: This Series II 88-inch model shows the cleaner, yet still purposeful, appearance of the restyled bodies.

Above: Later Series I Land-Rovers had this more comprehensive dashboard, which they passed on to the Series IIs and IIAs.
Above, right: With the Series IIA in 1961 came an enlarged diesel engine, now with the same 2¼-litre capacity as the petrol engine. Once again, this picture shows a later example, as fitted to Series III models.

Right: To meet the requirements of the British Army for an air-portable Land-Rover, Rover developed the the Half-Ton or Military Lightweight.
Below: The final Series IIA models can be identified by their combination of a mesh grille with wing-mounted headlamps.

Above: *Series III models shared basic styling with their predecessors. Instant recognition points, however, were the ABS plastic grille and the flat door hinges. This is an 88-inch model.*

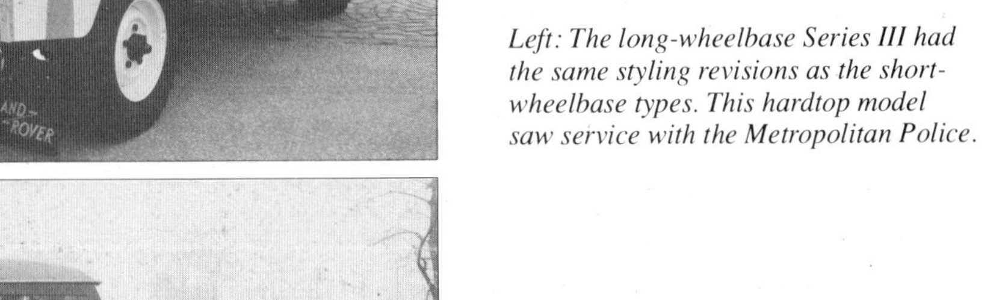

Left: The long-wheelbase Series III had the same styling revisions as the short-wheelbase types. This hardtop model saw service with the Metropolitan Police.

Left: The One-Ton Land-Rover was an uprated long-wheelbase model, introduced as a Series IIA in 1967. This is actually a Series III version. The larger tyres are an easy recognition point of the One-Ton models.

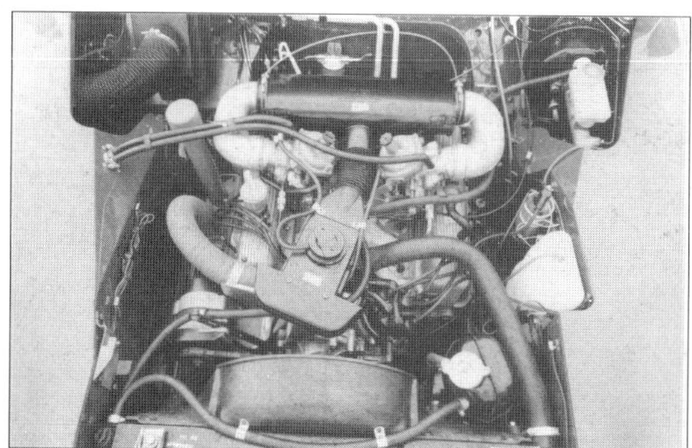

Above: The V8 engine in a Series III 'Stage I' V8 Land-Rover.

Right: A further-improved dashboard was a distinctive feature of Series III models.

Below: The V8-engined Series III models were easy to recognise, thanks to their revised front ends and side decal badging. They were the first new models to be announced by Land Rover Ltd after its formation in 1978.

Left: The market demanded higher trim and equipment levels in the early 1980s, and Land Rover Ltd responded with the County models. This is an 88-inch County Station Wagon.

Left: The improved interior of a County Station Wagon.

Left: Continued calls for more carrying capacity led to the development of the High-Capacity Pick-Up.

3. Choosing your Land-Rover

First and foremost, you need to establish exactly what you want a Land-Rover for. Most people buy one primarily for road use, though expecting it also to perform in less testing off-road conditions such as the mud of a farmyard or a construction site. Generally speaking, a long-wheelbase model will prove as able as a short-wheelbase one in these conditions. But if you really are looking for an off-road vehicle (and very few people are), then you are much better off with a short-wheelbase model — in fact, the shorter, the better. The long-wheelbase Land-Rovers are much more likely to catch their bellies on humps and ridges. Serious off-road trials enthusiasts simply don't rate long-wheelbase Land-Rovers, and you should follow their example.

It's well known that Land-Rovers make very good tow vehicles, but less well known that you really should have a long-wheelbase model for towing a big caravan or a car trailer: the short-wheelbase models don't have the stability for anything much bigger than a horse box or small, two-wheel trailer. It's also well-known that Land-Rovers make great load carriers, so if that's what you're after, make sure you settle for one with the payload and space you need. Lastly, if you want a Land-Rover for passenger-carrying duties, then you'll have to go for a Station Wagon. If you regularly carry a whole Scout Troop around, then you might well need a long-wheelbase model; otherwise, a short-wheelbase seven-seater provides ample space for most owners.

You'll also need to decide whether on-road performance or fuel economy is more important to you. It's quite true that a V8 109-inch will probably offer the best on-road performance of all the models surveyed here, but it's also true that you'll be looking at potentially crippling fuel bills. That's particularly so with the heavy Station Wagon body. The six-cylinder engines aren't all that frugal, either, and your best bet will almost certainly be a four-cylinder petrol engine. Still better fuel economy comes from the diesel engines, but you'll be looking at embarrassingly snail-like performance as well as noise levels which can be pretty wearing on a long journey.

No Land-Rover ever gained an award for extravagant creature comforts, but you need to know that some models are rather less refined than others. An early 80-inch vehicle can be enormous fun on a summer's day if you don't have far to drive, but you'll soon notice its shortcomings if you try a 300-mile round trip in the middle of winter. Essentially, if you worry about things like warmth and comfort, you'll be best going for a late Series III County Station Wagon or one of the professionally customised and rebuilt vehicles. Anything else is likely to prove a bit of a trial.

Lastly, a word of warning. An ex-military Land-Rover can prove a good buy, but beware of the so-called '24-volt' or 'FFR' (Fitted For Radio) vehicles. These have an electrical system designed to power additional electrical items which you will never need, and that system also differs from standard in several ways. Its components are expensive. If you must buy a 24-volt ex-military Land-Rover, get it converted to the standard 12-volt system as soon as you can!

Above: For stability in towing, a long-wheelbase model is the best bet.

Below: Some ex-military Land-Rovers have 24-volt electrical systems. The radio aerial tuner boxes on the front wings of the example closest to the camera are characteristic of such vehicles.

So you still want a Land-Rover? You might as well begin the process of choosing one by admitting to yourself that you are about to enter a minefield. The problem with this particular minefield is that no-one has bothered to leave any kind of map through it. What this Chapter is intended to do, then, is to give you a half-decent chance of getting through unscathed. But it's impossible to make any guarantees. Land-Rovers get used for so many different purposes that even experts occasionally come across something broken which they've never seen broken before.

To cut a long story short, you'll have to use a lot of your own judgement in buying a Land-Rover. Remember that they were never designed to be cossetted like cars, and that looking at a used example is not at all the same thing as looking at a desirable classic car. As a first step when assessing

LAND-ROVER BUYER'S CHECKLIST

However well-informed you may about the pitfalls of buying, it is easy when inspecting a superficially appealing vehicle to let enthusiasm get the better of caution and common sense. If necessary, take this checklist with you and make sure everything has been ticked off before you decide whether or not to purchase.

BODY
- condition and fit of panels
- hinge pillars
- door tops (Series II/IIA/III)
- bottom of door frames
- footwells
- bulkhead (Series I)

ENGINE
- leaks
- mountings
- tappet noise (IOE and V8)
- timing chain noise (OHV)
- oil fumes, smoke (diesel)

CHASSIS
- outriggers
- rear cross-member
- rear spring shackles (107/109)
- plating
- accident damage

SUSPENSION AND STEERING
- listing to one side
- broken/splayed springs
- hub swivels
- loose steering components
- steering kickback
- excessive wander

GEARBOX AND DRIVELINE
- jumping out of gear
- knocking noises
- engagement of 4WD and low ratio
- worn UJs
- worn differentials

BRAKES
- loose pipes
- pulling

a used example for sale, try to find out what the vehicle has been used for, because that can give you an idea of the sort of problems you might expect. One which has been used by a farmer to take his pigs to market might well be filthy and have an unlovable smell; but it might be preferable to the apparently well-preserved one which has spent its life pulling boats in and out of the sea and is now suffering from terminal salt-induced corrosion of the chassis.

Initial inspection

As will be clear from the other sections of this book, the construction of one Land-Rover is pretty much like the construction of another Land-Rover. That means that the faults which affect an early one are, broadly speaking, pretty similar to those which affect a late one. Where faults are specific to one model only, this guide says so. Otherwise, assume they apply to all models, early or late, short-wheelbase or long-wheelbase, petrol or diesel.

The first thing to do when examining a potential purchase is to make sure it is standing on level, hard ground. That way, any list to one side or another will be readily apparent. If the vehicle does list, it's probably got spring trouble. While at this stage of the assessment, you should walk all round the vehicle slowly and check whether the doors fit properly, whether all the panels fit properly, and whether there are any signs of major accident damage which has been hastily patched up. This overall assessment will give you some more ideas about what you should look at more closely later.

The bodywork and interior

While still outside the vehicle, begin your examination of its bodywork. The main body panels are made of aluminium alloy and should not show signs of corrosion. Nor should they bear gashes, whether mended or not. Dents and scrapes, however, are nothing to get too worried about. If you are looking at a Series III or late Series IIA model with the headlamps in the wings, check for corrosion of the bowls behind the lamps.

Next, open the doors. Look for rust in the bottoms of the hinge pillars (also visible below the door line on Series Is), in the panels surrounding the door windows on Series IIs, IIAs and IIIs, and in the steel frames at the bottoms of the doors. Get inside and check the footwells, which are notorious for rusting through. If you're looking at a Series I, give the bulkhead a thorough inspection: it can rust very badly. Trim is generally hard-wearing, although seat coverings do split. Series III 'County' seats, with their cloth coverings, are unlikely to show any damage other than soiling; if they do, remember that they are more expensive to replace than are other types.

The engine

The next thing to examine is the engine. As Land-Rovers are usually working vehicles, the engine bay itself is likely to be filthy, but that should not deter you: remember, different standards apply from those you might be used to for cars. The problem with a really dirty engine bay, however, is that you won't easily be able to detect oil and water leaks. You'll need a rag to help you wipe the muck off when you look at the vulnerable areas.

Check for water leaks from the radiator and hoses as a matter of course, and look below the water pump on all the four-cylinder and six-cylinder engines. Oil leaks, as you might expect, can come from the rocker covers or from the cylinder head joints on all Land-Rover engines. On V8s, watch out also for a lot of oil on the ground under the rear of the engine. This usually means that the rear main bearing oil seal is past its best and you might as well know that it's not an easy or quick job to replace it.

It might sound elementary, but you should also check the condition of the engine mountings. Land-Rovers often suffer a hard life, and it isn't uncommon to find broken engine mountings and severed or badly distorted rubbers. Refinement increases dramatically when such problems are rectified!

The petrol engines are all rugged, untemperamental pieces of machinery which seem to go on for ever. All of them should start easily, and all of them should settle down to an even tickover when warm. Remember that the same basic engines were used in Rover's high-quality saloon cars and that they were not designed to be rough, whatever some owners might say! However, many of them become rough in use, through neglect and through wear, and you need to be sure that any roughness in one you are looking at is easily rectifiable.

The IOE four-cylinder types often suffer from a light top-end knock, which might just be maladjusted tappet clearances but also might be worn cam followers (common in these engines) or a worn camshaft. On the six-cylinder engine, that same top-end knock generally has the same causes, although the cam followers were of an improved design and tend to last rather better. The OHV four-cylinder engine is actually rather rougher, even when in good condition, and often suffers from timing chain rattle. As Rover never cured this, you should not worry too much about it; but really bad timing-chain rattle suggests that the chain tensioner is unable to cope with the slack in the chain. This could lead to the chain jumping on the timing wheels, which in turn could cause valves to hit pistons.

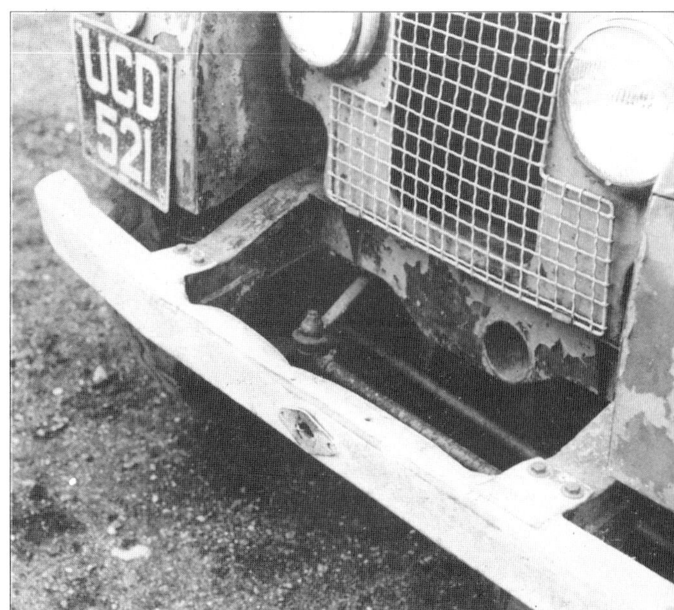

Above: Typical condition of a well-used Land-Rover, and easily rectifiable: the bumper is bolted to the chassis.

Above: This wing damage is also typical of the condition of an older Land-Rover.

Below: Gashes and tears in the alloy body panels might look bad, but at least they don't rust!

The V8 engines also have their characteristic noises. A general 'rustling' sound from the top end when the engine is warm usually means that the hydraulic tappets are beginning to wear and are failing to take up the clearances properly. Engines in this condition will carry on for many thousands of miles and need not cause you concern. However, a persistent top-end knock can warn of a worn camshaft, and general high noise usually means that the rockers are badly worn.

In spite of the reputation of modern diesel engines, the diesels fitted to the Series II and Series III Land-Rovers are often not as long-lived as the petrol types. Even in good condition, they create a lot of combustion 'knock'— the early 2-litre types particularly so. As they share the long timing chain of the OHV petrol types, they can also be noisy in this department, and for the same reasons. However, the best guide to wear in a diesel engine is to remove the crank case breather filter and to watch for fumes as you gradually increase engine speed. A lot of fumes, perhaps even accompanied by droplets of oil, mean a lot of wear.

Diesel engines start rather less readily than petrol types, and need about 30 seconds of pre-heating by their glow plugs before they will fire when cold. On start-up, you should watch for smoke from the exhaust. Some smoke is to be expected, but if the engine continues to produce large quantities when you open the throttle, then the injectors are probably either worn or badly adjusted. Persistent clouds of smoke at all engine speeds probably mean that the engine is very badly worn and possibly even has a cracked cylinder head.

Underneath

Before taking your potential purchase for a road-test, you need to have a careful look underneath. It is not true that all Land-Rovers have galvanised chassis frames and will never rust, whatever you may have heard. In fact, only the pre-production examples did so; the rest had frames of ordinary, rust-prone steel, and the fact that they are long-lived has more to do with the thickness of that steel than with any protection applied to it.

The chassis outriggers which support the body are notoriously prone to rust. However, replacements for these are cheap and fairly easy to fit. Rust on the rearmost cross member is also common, but rather more serious, as replacing the rear cross-member is a time-consuming job. Additionally, long-wheelbase models are prone to rusting around the rear spring shackles. While underneath, look also for ripples in the main side members where accident damage has been repaired, and treat with suspicion any large areas of plating on the chassis members: some owners try to save money in the short term by welding new metal over rust. Look, too, at the cross members under the clutch housing and gearbox. On a vehicle which has seen plenty of rough off-road use, these could be quite badly damaged. Wherever you suspect a problem, prod with a broad-bladed screwdriver. Any rust damage will soon become apparent.

While underneath, have a look at those parts of the running-gear which you can see. Check the springs for splaying and for broken leaves, and check too whether they have flattened out in use. If any of these faults are present, you'll have to think

Right: Small holes are often crudely repaired, like this.

Below: Look out for corrosion at the base of the door pillars on Series Is.

Right: Look for rust in the door frames…

Above: ...and remember that footwell rust, too, is very common.

of replacing the offending spring. Check the propshafts as well, by trying to twist them. Movement should be minimal, and excessive movement means worn universal joints, a condition which will be even more apparent on road-test when there will be severe vibration from the drive-train. You should also check for wear in the differentials. In this case, make sure the vehicle is chocked and release the hand brake. Then twist the propshafts again, first one way and then the other. If more than a quarter-turn is possible, there is enough wear in the appropriate differential to give you cause for concern.

At the outer ends of the front axle, examine the hub swivels — the large chromed balls emerging from the brake backplates. When new, they are chromium-plated and smooth, and they might leak a little oil. However, prolonged use of a Land-Rover in sand or gravel tends to result in corrosion and pitting of the chrome, which in turn destroys the oil seals and leads to more serious leaks. The hub swivels are expensive to replace. Protective leather gaiters were available as an optional extra and were fitted to all military Land-Rovers. Beware of suspiciously new-looking gaiters, though: they could have been put on to hide something.

Steering components are generally tough, but they can become damaged in off-road use. Steering boxes and relays often leak oil, but this need not be serious. More serious is the possibility of a steering box or relay working loose or coming adrift from its mountings. You should also check for looseness in the track rod ends and ball joints, though these can be replaced with new components fairly simply.

Brakes also need careful examination. There should be no fluid leakage around the back plates and the flexible hoses should show no signs of cracking or perishing close to a union. Similarly, all brake pipes should be properly attached to the chassis frame. Mountings can come adrift and leave a brake pipe hanging loose, leading to stress fractures or to the pipe being torn off completely, especially in off-road use.

Lastly, while underneath the vehicle, check for oil leaks which were not visible when you looked under the bonnet. A leaking rear main bearing seal on a V8 engine, for example, will be readily visible now. Don't forget to look at the gearbox and transfer box casings, too, for signs of leaks from these.

On the road

You should finish your inspection of a Land-Rover with a test drive. At this stage, you will be listening carefully for any odd noises which weren't apparent before, as well as watching for any odd behaviour from the engine or running gear. But, most of all, you will need to test the vehicle for transmission, steering and braking faults, as these will not show up in a static inspection.

As you select first gear, listen for the howling sound which a worn clutch release bearing will make. Once on the move, expect plenty of noise from the transmission, but listen for nasty grating noises. Some transmission shunt is inevitable with all those components in the driveline, but loud clonks as the drive is taken up or on the overrun mean that there is serious wear in the gearbox, transfer box or elsewhere in the driveline. In each gear, you should accelerate and then lift off the throttle suddenly, with your hand off the gear lever. If the selector then jumps out of mesh, there is unacceptable wear in the gearbox. Try it in reverse, too, and this time listen for knocking noises from the gearbox. These indicate chipped teeth in the gear train.

You should try a similar on-and-off the throttle test with four-wheel-drive and low ratio selected, and watch also for any reluctance of four-wheel-drive to disengage. Check the four-wheel-drive selector by depressing it on the move in high ratio. Then stop the vehicle and pull the red-knobbed lever back into low range. The lever with the yellow knob should pop up smartly if all is well.

All Land-Rovers tend to pull towards the kerb on a cambered road, so you should expect this. Similarly, the steering is none too precise and may cause the vehicle to weave a little over road surface irregularities. However, serious weaving means serious wear in steering components (or, possibly, worn or under-inflated tyres). Watch, too, for nasty kickback at the wheel as you encounter pot-holes: it probably means that the steering damper is past its best.

Lastly, try the brakes. If you try to stop the vehicle from high speed, you will undoubtedly frighten yourself, so it's best to go for a moderate speed like 40mph prior to your test stop. The Land-Rover should pull up all-square. The vehicle might sway a little on its suspension, but it should definitely not weave or pull to one side.

Above: Land-Rover seats have a hard time and are often split or torn. These are on a Series III model.

Below: Look for signs of water leakage below the water-pump.

Left: If a diesel engine fumes excessively from the crankcase breather tube, it's probably on its last legs. The breather cap has been removed in this picture, for clarity.

Above: The Land-Rover has a tough chassis, but its outriggers are only too prone to corrosion, as this example shows.

Left: Rear cross-members are another rust-prone area of the Land-Rover chassis...

Right: ...and you should also check for rust around the rear spring shackles on long-wheelbase models.

Below: Not all chassis repairs are carried out to the highest standards, and you should look for evidence of crude plating. This outrigger has in fact been repaired rather well.

Right: You won't often find one that has been bent this badly! The best solution in such cases is to replace the chassis. For this Series III (though not for earlier models), a chassis frame is available from Land Rover Parts.

Above: The bulkhead can rot very badly on early vehicles. Remanufactured items for some models are available from specialists.

Left: It is possible to fit front wings from an 86-inch or 107-inch model to the later 88-inch and 109-inch types. This shows what happens if you do!

Below: A neat repair has been made around this door hinge. But why did it need to be plated in the first place? Is there still some untreated rust lurking in the A-pillar somewhere?

4. Facts and figures

Identifying a Land-Rover

The easiest way of identifying what sort of Land-Rover you are looking at is by examining the chassis number plate. Where to look for that depends on the age of the vehicle.

On *early Series I* models, it is found in two places: under the bonnet, on a brass plate fixed to the left-hand-side of the bulkhead, and stamped on the left-hand engine mounting, under the bonnet.

Later Series Is (86-inch and 107-inch models) have the chassis number plate on the bulkhead inside the vehicle and on the left-hand rear spring hanger.

88-inch and 109-inch models also have a plate on the bulkhead inside, but the number is repeated on the right-hand front spring hanger.

Series IIA and Series III models have the number on a plate fixed to the bulkhead just above the gearbox cover inside the vehicle.

Lastly, *military models* generally have one plate on the bulkhead inside and a second on the side of the front seat box.

Chassis numbers

Seven different chassis numbering systems were used for the Land-Rovers covered by this book. In all cases, the last five numbers (four before 1950) are the vehicle's serial number and do not affect identification of its type.

Type identification is established from the first group of numbers in an all-numeric chassis number. The type codes are as follows (all dates given are for model-year). Note that additional type-codes were allocated to CKD vehicles, but the absence of records makes it impossible to be certain whether examples were built in these number series.

0610 1950 80-inch, basic and CKD;
. . . . . . preceded by R or L for RHD or LHD
0620 1950 80-inch, Station Wagon;
. . . . . . preceded by R or L for RHD or LHD
0630 1950 80-inch, Welder;
. . . . . . preceded by R or L for RHD or LHD
0710 1950 80-inch, 2-litre prototype batch;
. . . . . . preceded by R or L for RHD or LHD
86 1948-1949 80-inch, basic and CKD (first 3,000 vehicles only);
. . . . . . preceded by R or L for RHD or LHD
222 Series IIA 109-inch 1-ton, 6-cyl petrol, RHD export
223 . . . . LHD export
229 . . . . home market
231 Series IIA 109-inch 1-ton, 4-cyl petrol, home market
236 Series IIA 88-inch ½-ton, 4-cyl petrol, military lightweight,
. . . . home market
239 . . . . LHD export
241 Series IIA 88-inch petrol, home market
(also Station Wagons to March 1965)
242 . . . . RHD export
243 . . . . RHD, CKD
244 . . . . LHD export
245 . . . . LHD, CKD
251 Series IIA 109-inch 4-cyl petrol, home market

252 . . . . RHD export
253 . . . . RHD, CKD
254 . . . . LHD export
255 . . . . LHD, CKD
259 Series III 88-inch Station Wagon, 4-cyl petrol, LHD for USA
261 Series IIA 109-inch Station Wagon, 4-cyl petrol, home market (see also 2610; Series IIA numbers end with a suffix letter)
262 . . . . RHD export
263 . . . . RHD, CKD (see also 2630; Series IIA numbers end with a suffix letter)
264 . . . . LHD export
265 . . . . LHD, CKD
266 Series III 109-inch 1-ton, 6-cyl petrol, home market
267 . . . . RHD export
269 . . . . LHD export
271 Series IIA 88-inch diesel, home market (also Station Wagons to March 1965)
272 . . . . RHD export
273 . . . . RHD, CKD
274 . . . . LHD export
275 . . . . LHD, CKD
276 Series IIA 109-inch diesel, home market
277 . . . . RHD export
278 . . . . RHD, CKD
279 . . . . LHD export
280 . . . . LHD, CKD
281 Series IIA 109-inch diesel Station Wagon, home market
282 . . . . RHD export
283 . . . . RHD, CKD
284 . . . . LHD export
285 . . . . LHD, CKD
286 Series IIa 109-inch Forward Control, 4-cyl petrol, home market
287 . . . . RHD export
288 . . . . RHD, CKD
289 . . . . LHD export
290 . . . . LHD, CKD
300 Series IIA 109-inch Forward Control, 6-cyl petrol, home market
301 . . . . RHD export
302 . . . . RHD, CKD
303 . . . . LHD export
304 . . . . LHD, CKD
305 Series IIA 109-inch Forward Control, diesel, home market
310 Series IIA 109-inch military, airportable
315 Series IIA 88-inch Station Wagon, 4-cyl petrol, home market . . . . (from March 1965)
316 . . . . RHD export
318 . . . . LHD export
320 Series IIA 88-inch Station Wagon, diesel, home market . . . . (from March 1965)
321 . . . . RHD export
323 . . . . LHD export
325 Series IIB 110-inch Forward Control, 4-cyl petrol, home market
326 . . . . RHD export
328 . . . . LHD export
330 Series IIB 110-inch Forward Control, 6-cyl petrol, home market
331 . . . . RHD export
333 . . . . LHD export
335 Series IIB 110-inch Forward Control, diesel, home market
336 . . . . RHD export
338 . . . . LHD export
343 Series IIA 109-inch Station Wagon, LHD for USA
345 Series IIA 109-inch, 6-cyl petrol, home market
346 . . . . RHD export
348 . . . . LHD export

350	Series IIA 109-inch Station Wagon, 6-cyl petrol, home market	
351	. . . .	RHD export
353	. . . .	LHD export
866	1949 80-inch, basic and CKD; preceded by R or L for RHD or LHD	
867	1949 80-inch, Station Wagon; preceded by R or L for RHD or LHD	
868	1949 80-inch, Welder; preceded by R or L for RHD or LHD	
895	Series III 88-inch ½-ton, diesel, military lightweight,	
	. . . .	LHD export
901	Series III 88-inch petrol, home market	
902	. . . .	RHD export
904	. . . .	LHD export
906	Series III 88-inch diesel, home market	
907	. . . .	RHD export
909	. . . .	LHD export
911	Series III 109-inch, 4-cyl petrol, home market	
912	. . . .	RHD export
914	. . . .	LHD export
916	Series III 109-inch diesel, home market	
917	. . . .	RHD export
919	. . . .	LHD export
921	Series III 88-inch petrol, Station Wagon, home market	
922	. . . .	RHD oxport
924	. . . .	LHD export
926	Series III 88-inch diesel, Station Wagon, home market	
927	. . . .	RHD export
929	. . . .	LHD export
931	Series III 109-inch, 4-cyl petrol, Station Wagon, home market	
932	. . . .	RHD export

Above: The chassis number of a Series I can be found on the chassis rail beside the engine mounting…

Below: ….and on a plate on the engine side of the bulkhead.

Above: Series II, IIA and III models have the chassis number on a plate above the bell-housing on the passenger compartment side of the bulkhead.

Below: The Military Lightweight's chassis plate is located on the bulkhead, outboard of the steering column.

934		. . . . LHD export
936		Series III 109-inch diesel, Station Wagon, home market
937		. . . . RHD export
939		. . . . LHD export
941		Series III 109-inch, 6-cyl petrol, home market
942		. . . . RHD export
944		. . . . LHD export
946		Series III 109-inch, 6-cyl petrol, Station Wagon, home market
947		. . . . RHD export
949		. . . . LHD export
951		Series III 88-inch ½-ton petrol, military lightweight, home market
952		. . . . RHD export
954		. . . . LHD export
956		101-inch Forward Control (12-volt), home market
957		. . . . RHD export
959		. . . . LHD export
961		. . . . (24-volt), home market
962		. . . . RHD export
964		. . . . LHD export
1116	1956	88-inch, petrol, basic and Station Wagon, home market
1117	1957	. . . .
1118	1958	. . . .
1126	1956	88-inch, petrol, basic and Station Wagon, RHD export
1127	1957	. . . .
1128	1958	. . . .
1136	1956	88-inch, petrol, basic and Station Wagon, RHD, CKD
1137	1957	. . . .
1138	1958	. . . .

1146	1956	88-inch, petrol, basic and Station Wagon, LHD export
1147	1957	. . . .
1148	1958	. . . .
1156	1956	88-inch, petrol, basic and Station Wagon, LHD, CKD
1157	1957	. . . .
1158	1958	. . . .
1166	1956	88-inch, diesel, basic and Station Wagon, home market
1167	1957	. . . .
1168	1958	. . . .
1176	1956	88-inch, diesel, basic and Station Wagon, RHD export
1177	1957	. . . .
1178	1958	. . . .
1186	1956	88-inch, diesel, basic and Station Wagon, RHD, CKD
1187	1957	. . . .
1188	1958	. . . .
1196	1956	88-inch, diesel, basic and Station Wagon, LHD export
1197	1957	. . . .
1198	1958	. . . .
1206	1956	88-inch, diesel, basic and Station Wagon, LHD, CKD
1207	1957	. . . .
1208	1958	. . . .
1216	1956	109-inch, petrol, home market
1217	1957	. . . .
1218	1958	. . . .
1226	1956	109-inch, petrol, RHD export
1227	1957	. . . .
1228	1958	. . . .
1236	1956	109-inch, petrol, RHD, CKD
1237	1957	. . . .
1238	1958	. . . .
1246	1956	109-inch, petrol, LHD export
1247	1957	. . . .
1248	1958	. . . .
1256	1956	109-inch, petrol, LHD, CKD
1257	1957	. . . .
1258	1958	. . . .
1266	1956	109-inch, diesel, home market
1267	1957	. . . .
1268	1958	. . . .
1276	1956	109-inch, diesel, RHD export
1277	1957	. . . .
1278	1958	. . . .
1286	1956	109-inch, diesel, RHD, CKD
1287	1957	. . . .
1288	1958	. . . .
1296	1956	109-inch, diesel, LHD export
1297	1957	. . . .
1298	1958	. . . .
1306	1956	109-inch, diesel, LHD, CKD
1307	1957	. . . .
1308	1958	. . . .
1317	1957	107-inch Station Wagon, home market
1318	1958	. . . .
1327	1957	107-inch Station Wagon, RHD export
1328	1958	. . . .
1337	1957	107-inch Station Wagon, RHD, CKD
1338	1958	. . . .
1347	1957	107-inch Station Wagon, LHD export
1348	1958	. . . .
1357	1957	107-inch Station Wagon, LHD, CKD
1358	1958	. . . .
1410	1960	88-inch Series II, petrol, basic and Station Wagon, home market
1411	1961	. . . .
1418	1958	. . . .
1419	1959	. . . .
1420	1960	88-inch Series II, petrol, basic and Station Wagon, RHD export
1421	1961	. . . .
1428	1958	. . . .
1429	1959	. . . .
1430	1960	88-inch Series II, petrol, basic and Station Wagon, RHD, CKD
1431	1961	. . . .
1438	1958	. . . .
1439	1959	. . . .
1440	1960	88-inch Series II, petrol, basic and Station Wagon, LHD export
1441	1961	. . . .
1448	1958	. . . .
1449	1959	. . . .
1450	1960	88-inch Series II, petrol, basic and Station Wagon, LHD, CKD
1451	1961	. . . .
1458	1958	. . . .
1459	1959	. . . .
1460	1960	88-inch Series II, diesel, basic and Station Wagon, home market

1461 1961 . . . .
1468 1958 . . . .
1469 1959 . . . .
1470 1960 88-inch Series II, diesel, basic and Station Wagon, RHD export
1471 1961 . . . .
1478 1958 . . . .
1479 1959 . . . .
1480 1960 88-inch Series II, diesel, basic and Station Wagon, RHD, CKD
1481 1961 . . . .
1488 1958 . . . .
1489 1959 . . . .
1490 1960 88-inch Series II, diesel, basic and Station Wagon, LHD export
1491 1961 . . . .
1498 1958 . . . .
1499 1959 . . . .

1500 1960 88-inch Series II, diesel, basic and Station Wagon, LHD, CKD
1501 1961 . . . .
1508 1958 . . . .
1509 1959 . . . .
1510 1960 109-inch petrol, home market
1511 1961 . . . .
1518 1958 . . . .
1519 1959
1520 1960 109-inch petrol, RHD export
1521 1961 . . . .
1528 1958 . . . .
1529 1959 . . . .
1530 1960 109-inch petrol, RHD, CKD
1531 1961 . . . .
1538 1958 . . . .
1539 1959 . . . .
1540 1960 109-inch petrol, LHD export
1541 1961 . . . .
1548 1958 . . . .
1549 1959 . . . .
1550 1960 109-inch petrol, LHD, CKD
1551 1961 . . . .
1558 1958 . . . .
1559 1959 . . . .
1560 1960 109-inch diesel, home market
1561 1961 . . . .
1568 1958 . . . .
1569 1959 . . . .
1570 1960 109-inch diesel, RHD export
1571 1961 . . . .
1578 1958 . . . .
1579 1959 . . . .
1580 1960 109-inch diesel, RHD, CKD
1581 1961 . . . .
1588 1958 . . . .
1589 1959 . . . .
1590 1960 109-inch diesel, LHD export
1591 1961 . . . .
1598 1958 . . . .
1599 1959 . . . .

1600 1960 109-inch diesel, LHD, CKD
1601 1961 . . . .
1608 1958 . . . .
1609 1959 . . . .
1610 (8-digit number) 1951 80-inch, home market
1610 (9-digit number) 1960 109-inch petrol, Station Wagon, home market
1611 1961 109-inch petrol, Station Wagon, home market
1613 1951 80-inch, LHD export
1616 1951 80-inch, RHD export
1619 1959 109-inch petrol, Station Wagon, home market
1620 (8-digit number) 1951 80-inch Station Wagon, home market
1620 (9-digit number) 1960 109-inch petrol, Station Wagon, RHD export
1621 1961 109-inch petrol, Station Wagon, RHD export
1623 1951 80-inch Station Wagon, LHD export
1626 1951 80-inch Station Wagon, RHD export
1629 1959 109-inch petrol, Station Wagon, RHD export
1630 (8-digit number) 1951 80-inch, Welder, home market
1630 (9-digit number) 1960 109-inch petrol, Station Wagon, RHD, CKD
1631 1961 109-inch petrol, Station Wagon, RHD, CKD
1633 1951 80-inch, Welder, LHD export
1636 1951 80-inch, Welder, RHD export
1639 1959 109-inch petrol, Station Wagon, RHD, CKD
1640 1960 109-inch petrol, Station Wagon, LHD export
1641 1961 . . . .
1649 1959 . . . .
1650 1960 109-inch petrol, Station Wagon, LHD, CKD
1651 1961 . . . .
1659 1959 . . . .
1660 1960 109-inch diesel, Station Wagon, home market
1661 1961 . . . .
1663 1951 80-inch, LHD, CKD
1666 1951 80-inch, RHD, CKD
1669 1959 109-inch diesel, Station Wagon, home market
1670 1960 109-inch diesel, Station Wagon, RHD export
1671 1961 . . . .
1679 1959 . . . .
1680 1960 109-inch diesel, Station Wagon, RHD, CKD
1681 1961 . . . .
1689 1959 . . . .
1690 1960 109-inch diesel, Station Wagon, LHD export
1691 1961 . . . .
1699 1959 . . . .

1700 1960 109-inch diesel, Station Wagon, LHD, CKD
1701 1961 . . . .
1706 1956 86-inch, home market
1709 1959 109-inch diesel, Station Wagon, LHD, CKD
1736 1956 86-inch, LHD export
1746 1956 86-inch, LHD, CKD
1766 1956 86-inch, RHD export
1776 1956 86-inch, RHD, CKD

2610 1952 80-inch, home market (see also 261; 1952 models have no suffix letter)
2613 1952 80-inch, LHD export
2616 1952 80-inch, RHD export
2630 1952 80-inch, Welder, home market (see also 263; 1952 models have no suffix letter)

VIN numbers

From 1st November 1979, all Land-Rovers had standardised VIN numbers, initially with 8 letters and later with 11 preceding the serial number. All V8 models, including those built before November 1979, had VIN codes.
All 11-number codes begin with SAL, which simply identifies the manufacturer as Land Rover Ltd.
The **fourth digit** (first in 8-digit numbers) is always L and identifies the model as Land-Rover (i.e. as distinct from Range Rover).
The **fifth to eighth digits** decode as follows:

BAAH	88-inch petrol
BAAG	88-inch diesel
BABH	88-inch Station Wagon, petrol
BABG	88-inch Station Wagon, diesel
BCAH	109-inch, 4-cyl petrol
BCAG	109-inch diesel
BCAP	109-inch, 6-cyl petrol
BCAV	109-inch, V8 petrol
BCMH	109-inch Station Wagon, 4-cyl petrol
BCMG	109-inch Station Wagon, diesel
BCMP	109-inch Station Wagon, 6-cyl petrol
BCMV	109-inch Station Wagon, V8 petrol
BDAH	109-inch 1-ton, 4-cyl petrol
BDAP	109-inch 1-ton, 6-cyl petrol

The **ninth and tenth digits** represent steering and transmission types:

1A RHD, four-speed
2A LHD, four-speed

The **eleventh digit** indicates the type of manufacture:

A	fully built at Solihull
F	CKD vehicle for overseas assembly

2633	1952	80-inch, Welder, LHD export
2636	1952	80-inch, Welder, RHD export
2663	1952	80-inch, LHD, CKD
2666	1952	80-inch, RHD, CKD
2706	1956	107-inch, home market
2736	1956	107-inch, LHD export
2746	1956	107-inch, LHD, CKD
2766	1956	107-inch, RHD export
2776	1956	107-inch, RHD, CKD
3610	1953	80-inch, home market
3613	1953	80-inch, LHD export
3616	1953	80-inch, RHD export
3630	1953	80-inch, Welder, home market
3633	1953	80-inch, Welder, LHD export
3636	1953	80-inch, Welder, RHD export
3663	1953	80-inch, LHD, CKD
3666	1953	80-inch, RHD, CKD
4710	1954	86-inch, home market
4713	1954	86-inch, LHD export
4716	1954	86-inch, RHD export
4720	1954	107-inch, home market
4723	1954	107-inch, LHD export
4726	1954	107-inch, RHD export
4763	1954	86-inch, LHD, CKD
4766	1954	86-inch, RHD, CKD
4773	1954	107-inch, LHD, CKD
4776	1954	107-inch, RHD, CKD
5710	1955	86-inch, home market
5713	1955	86-inch, LHD export
5716	1955	86-inch, RHD export
5720	1955	107-inch, home market
5723	1955	107-inch, LHD export
5726	1955	107-inch, RHD export
5763	1955	86-inch, LHD, CKD
5766	1955	86-inch, RHD, CKD
5773	1955	107-inch, LHD, CKD
5776	1955	107-inch, RHD, CKD
8706	1956	107-inch Station Wagon, home market
8736	1956	107-inch Station Wagon, LHD export
8746	1956	107-inch Station Wagon, LHD, CKD
8766	1956	107-inch Station Wagon, RHD export
8776	1956	107-inch Station Wagon, RHD, CKD

LAND-ROVER TECHNICAL SPECIFICATIONS

(All dates refer to model-year.)

SERIES I 80-INCH MODELS

Engine:

(a) 1948-1951. 1,595cc (69.5mm x 105mm) four-cylinder petrol, overhead inlet and side exhaust valves. Compression ratio 6.8:1. Solex carburettor. Three-bearing crankshaft. 50bhp @ 4,000rpm; 80 lbs/ft @ 2,000rpm.

(b) 1952-1953.1,997cc (77.8mm x 105mm) four-cylinder petrol, overhead inlet and side exhaust valves. Compression ratio 6.8:1. Solex carburettor. Three-bearing crankshaft. 52bhp @ 4,000rpm; 101 lbs/ft @ 1,500rpm.

Transmission: (a) 1948-1950. Permanent four-wheel-drive with freewheel in front driveline. Single dry plate clutch. Four-speed gearbox with synchromesh on 3rd and 4th only; ratios 3.00:1, 2.04:1, 1.47:1, 1.1:1, reverse 2.54:1. Transfer gearbox giving 1.148:1 step-down ratio in High range and 2.89:1 in Low range. Final drive ratio 4.7:1 (very early vehicles have a 4.88:1 final drive)

(b) 1950-1953. Selectable four-wheel or two-wheel (rear) drive in High range only; permanent four-wheel drive in Low range. No freewheel in front driveline. Third gear now 1.38:1.

Steering, Suspension and Brakes:

Recirculating-ball, worm-and-nut steering with 15:1 ratio. Live axles front and rear with semi-elliptic leaf springs and telescopic dampers. Drum brakes at the wheels and mechanical transmission brake.

Dimensions: Wheelbase 80in. Front and rear tracks 50in. Length 132in. Width 61in. Height (hood up) 70.5in (1948-1951); 73.5in (1952-1954).

SERIES I 86-INCH MODELS

As for 1952-1953 80-inch models, except:

Engine: (a) 1954. As for 1952-1953 80-inch models.

(b) 1955-1956. Revised cylinder block with water between all bores.

Other specifications as before.

Dimensions: Wheelbase 86in. Length 140.7in. Height (hood up) 76in.

SERIES I 107-INCH MODELS

As for 86-inch models, except:

Dimensions: Wheelbase 107in. Length 173.5in. Width 62.5in. Height (hood up) 83.5in; height of Station Wagon 78in.

SERIES I 88-INCH MODELS

As for 86-inch models, except:

Engine: 1957-1958. Alternative 2,052cc (85.7mm x 88.9mm) four-cylinder diesel, OHV. Compression ratio 22.5:1. Indirect injection. Three-bearing crankshaft. 51bhp @ 3,500rpm; 87 lbs/ft @ 2,000rpm.

Dimensions: Wheelbase 88in. Length 140.75in. Width 62.6in.

SERIES I 109-INCH MODELS

As for 88-inch models, except:

Dimensions: Wheelbase 109in. Length 173.5in. Height (hood up) 83.5in.

LAND-ROVER TECHNICAL SPECIFICATIONS

SERIES II 88-INCH MODELS

As for 88-inch Series I, except:

Engine: (a) 2,286cc (90.47mm x 88.9mm) four-cylinder petrol, OHV. Compression ratio 7.0:1. Solex carburettor. Three-bearing crankshaft. 77bhp @ 4,250rpm; 124 lbs/ft @ 2,500rpm.
(b) 2,052cc diesel as in 88-inch Series I.

Dimensions: Front and rear tracks: 51.5in. Length 142.4in. Width 64in. Maximum height 77.5in.

SERIES II 109-INCH MODELS

As for 88-inch Series II, except:

Dimensions: Wheelbase 109in. Length 175in. Maximum height 81in.

SERIES IIA 88-INCH MODELS

As for 88-inch Series II, except:

Engine: (a) 2,286cc petrol engine with Zenith carburettor in place of Solex from 1967.
(b) 2,286cc (90.47mm x 88.9mm) four-cylinder diesel, OHV. Compression ratio 23:1. Indirect injection. Three-bearing crankshaft. 62bhp @ 4,000rpm; 103 lbs/ft @ 1,800rpm.

Transmission: From 1967, gear ratios 3.60:1, 2.22:1, 1.50:1, 1:1, reverse 3.02:1; transfer box Low range step-down 2.35:1.

SERIES IIA 109-INCH MODELS

As for 88-inch Series IIA, except:

Engine: From 1967, optional 2,625cc (77.8mm x 105mm) six-cylinder petrol, overhead inlet and side exhaust valves. Compression ratio 7.8:1. Zenith carburettor (very early models had an SU carburettor). Seven-bearing crankshaft. 83bhp @ 4,500rpm; 128 lbs/ft @ 1,500rpm.

Dimensions: Wheelbase 109in. Length 175in. Maximum height 81in.

SERIES IIA 109-INCH 1-TON MODELS

As for 109-inch Series IIA, except:

Engine: Six-cylinder or four-cylinder petrol engines only.

Transmission: Transfer box with 1.53:1 step-down ratio in High range and 3.27:1 step-down ratio in Low range.

SERIES III 88-INCH MODELS

As for 88-inch Series IIA, except:

Engine: From 1980, five-bearing crankshaft in four-cylinder petrol and diesel engines.

Transmission: Synchromesh on all forward gears. First gear ratio 3.68:1 (later 3.73:1), reverse 4.02:1. Overdrive with 0.782:1 ratio optional from August 1974.

Brakes: Servo-assistance standard on Station Wagons, optional on other models.

Dimensions: Length 142.6in. Width 66in. Maximum height 77in.

SERIES III 109-INCH MODELS

As for 88-inch Series III, except:

Engine: 1971-1980. Six-cylinder petrol engine had 86bhp @ 4,500rpm; 132 lbs/ft @ 1,500rpm. This engine discontinued, 1980.

Brakes: Servo-assistance standard on all six-cylinder and Station Wagon models; optional on others.

Dimensions: Wheelbase 109in. Length 173.5in. Front and rear tracks 52.5in. Maximum height 79in.

LAND-ROVER TECHNICAL SPECIFICATIONS

SERIES III 109-INCH 1-TON MODELS

As for 109-inch Series III, except:

Engine: Six-cylinder petrol only available.

Transmission: Transfer box with 1.53:1 step-down ratio in High range and 3.27:1 step-down ratio in Low range.

Brakes: Servo-assistance standard.

SERIES III 109-INCH V8 MODELS

As for 109-inch Series III, except:

Engine: 3,528cc (88.9mm x 71.1mm) V8 petrol, OHV. Compression ratio 8.13:1. Two Zenith-Stromberg carburettors. Five-bearing crankshaft. 91bhp @ 3,500rpm; 166 lbs/ft @ 2,000rpm.

Transmission: Permanent four-wheel drive with lockable centre differential. Gear ratios 4.069:1, 2.448:1, 1.505:1, 1:1, reverse 3.664:1; transfer box with 1.336:1 step-down ratio in High range and 3.321:1 step-down ratio in Low range. Final drive ratio 3.54:1.

Brakes: Servo-assistance standard.

PRODUCTION FIGURES

Series I			
	80-inch	1.6-litre	39,879
	80-inch	2-litre	37,801
	86-inch		49,342
	107-inch		27,346
	88-inch		39,992
	109-inch		23,967
Series II			
	88-inch		60,463
	109-inch		49,611
Series IIA			
	88-inch		151,813
	109-inch	all types	191,485
Series III			
	88-inch	Figures not available*	
	109-inch	Figures not available*	

* The total figure for Series III models is given by Land-Rover Ltd as 250,000.

PERFORMANCE FIGURES

Note: Figures vary greatly, depending on bodywork type. These are average maximum mph/fuel consumption mpg figures for "standard" vehicles.

		Maximum mph	*Fuel consumption mpg*
Series I	80-inch 1.6-litre	55	27
	80-inch 2-litre	60	23
	86-inch	60	22
	107-inch	58	18
	88-inch petrol	60	22
	88-inch diesel	55	30
	109-inch petrol	58	18
	109-inch diesel	53	27
Series II	88-inch petrol	70	18
	88-inch diesel	62	30
	109-inch petrol	68	16
	109-inch diesel	60	27
Series IIA	88-inch petrol	70	18
	88-inch diesel	60	27
	109-inch petrol (4-cyl.)	68	16
	109-inch petrol (6-cyl.)	73	15
	109-inch diesel	59	26
Series III	88-inch petrol	70	18
	88-inch diesel	60	27
	109-inch petrol (4-cyl.)	68	16
	109-inch petrol (6-cyl.)	73	15
	109-inch petrol (V8)	76	17
	109-inch diesel	60	27

LAND ROVER
AG 10347 U

Top: Perhaps the ideal starting point for building a Land-Rover to meet your needs is an ex-military vehicle, in this case a 109-inch Series III window hard top, sold through Brooklyn Engineering.

Above: Winches are common accessories but do you really need one?

Right: Freewheel hubs are a worthwhile accessory, which can save fuel as well as saving wear and tear on the drivetrain. They must be locked before engaging four-wheel-drive.

5. Modified Land-Rovers

Land-Rovers are working vehicles and, as such, they lose their *raison d'être* if they are not perfectly adapted to the tasks they are expected to perform. Whereas a car may be forgiven a few foibles because it is also a status symbol, a Land-Rover is a tool.

From the very beginning, then, Land-Rovers have been modified. The farmers who bought the earliest examples were no respecters of 'original specification' and, if they wanted the vehicle to do something for which it was not already suitable, they simply modified it so that it would. That tradition continues today, and modifications are an essential part of the Land-Rover scene. Of course, there *are* Land-Rover enthusiasts who want their vehicles to stay exactly the way they were when they left the factory; but they are few and far between. Most Land-Rovers you will find for sale will have been modified in one way or another at some time in their lives.

Under the heading of modifications, we must include what would nowadays be called 'bolt-on goodies'. As the Rover Company (and, later, Land Rover Ltd) was for many years too busy trying to meet demand for the basic vehicles to worry about offering all the extras which customers wanted, a large parasite industry grew up to fill the gap. If the customers wanted it, someone, somehere, would manufacture it. Sometimes, items would be submitted for Land Rover approval, but there were many which were not. These 'non-factory' items included many expedition accessories, winches, extra seats, and so on.

It would also be impossible to discuss modified Land-Rovers without mentioning factory-approved conversions — vehicles converted outside Solihull when they were new to specifications approved by Land Rover. These range from ambulances and fire engines to security vans and breakdown trucks, from crop-sprayers and mobile caravans to armoured cars and missile launch platforms. Some Land-Rovers have been converted to six-wheelers, and some have been converted to run on crawler tracks. The range is infinite, and is really outside the scope of this guide. Such vehicles will be found for sale from time to time, however, and prospective purchasers will have to judge each case on its merits.

Bodywork

The bolted-together construction of the Land-Rover's body makes modifications relatively easy to achieve. It is quite possible, for example, to turn a long-wheelbase pick-up into a long-wheelbase Station Wagon simply by unbolting one body and bolting on the other — though those who have tried it will tell you it isn't *quite* as straightforward as it might sound!

Much more common than this sort of major conversion is the simple construction of a wooden dropside rear body or a van top on a pick-up. As there are so many different possibilites, you will have to make your own mind up about the merits or otherwise of a vehicle like this which comes up for sale. Probably the best criterion to apply in all cases is the one of construction quality. Quite often, home-built conversions are not very robust!

Left: An overdrive unit is simple to fit and can save you fuel. Do your sums first, though. How long will it take you to recoup the cost of fitting the overdrive?

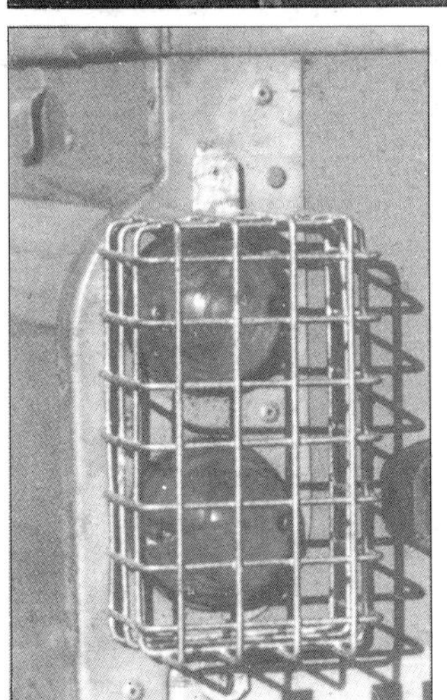

Below and bottom: Mesh lamp guards are a worthwhile addition if you use your Land-Rover off-road a lot, because they prevent damage to the lights from trees and bushes.

You will also come across oddities in your search for a Land-Rover. It is quite possible, for example, to bolt the front wings from an 86-inch Land Rover on to an 80-inch model; or to bolt the front wings from an 88-inch on to an 86-inch. There are differences, of course, but almost anything can be made to fit with patience! A quite common modification is to fit the latest (90/110/Defender) front end on to an earlier vehicle. Only you can say whether the fact that the specification is 'wrong' matters to you.

Engines

Even though Land-Rover engines are pretty robust pieces of machinery, they tend to wear out before the bodies and chassis into which they are fitted. When the time comes to fit a new engine, owners have often preferred to fit a more powerful one than the original. You will, therefore, find many Land-Rovers with non-original engines.

Starting at the beginning, it is perfectly possible to fit a 2-litre petrol engine in place of the earlier 1.6-litre type. The original 2-litre diesels were not the most powerful or the most refined of engines and many owners took advantage of the fact that the later 2.25-litre type could be substituted without difficulty. 2.25-litre diesels are interchangeable with 2.25-litre petrol engines and, of course, the post-1980 five-bearing types can be fitted in place of the original three-bearing types. It's also possible to fit the later 2.5-litre petrol and diesel engines in place of the 2.25-litre types! And specialists have offered bolt-on turbochargers for the diesel engines since the early 1980s.

As the early diesel engines made the Land-Rover rather slow, especially when fitted in the heavier long-wheelbase models, many owners looked for alternative diesel power units. Favourites have been Perkins engines of various sorts, and these are long-lasting and reliable. Also quite common is the BMC 2.2-litre diesel formerly used in Austin taxis. But vibration can be a problem with a diesel engine, especially if it has not been fitted very well. If you're thinking of buying a Land-Rover with a non-standard diesel conversion, check what it feels like both at a low-speed crawl and at maximum revs on the road. Weaknesses in the fabrication of home-made engine mountings will soon show up!

Generally speaking, however, engine swaps like these will have been carried out on vehicles which work for their living. Land-Rovers which have passed through the hands of enthusiasts are very often modified with more powerful engines, and the favourite of them all is the Rover V8. As often as not, this is used in car or Range Rover tune to give a hefty dollop of extra performance. On a vehicle which has been modified to run a V8, though, it's worth checking whether the brakes and suspension have been uprated to suit. One reason why the V8 was originally offered only in long-wheelbase models and in a low state of tune was that the brakes and suspension of the 88-inch simply weren't up to coping with the extra performance.

Even Rover tried out Land-Rovers equipped with the OHC four-cylinder engine from their P6 saloons. They didn't put them into production, but the experience of those who have done the conversion at home suggests that shortage of money was more likely to have been the reason than any problems with the conversion itself. The best of the engines for Land Rover use is the 2.2-litre

Left: Eight-spoke wheels are a popular custom accessory for Land-Rovers of all ages.

Below: Side stripes? Some people like them, others don't. This long-wheelbase Series I certainly gets noticed: it has orange stripes on a yellow body, and a blue canvas tilt!

Left: Some owners have converted vehicles to suit their own requirements. This mobile caravan started life as an ambulance.

Right: Others have carried out more radical transformations, as this caravan body on a long-wheelbase chassis shows. The picture was taken at a rally held in 1986 to protest against Government plans to sell Land Rover Ltd to a foreign buyer, which explains the presence of the "Keep Land Rover British" stickers.

Right: Much simpler is to buy a fully refurbished vehicle from one of the specialists. This 88-inch Series III was refurbished by the Land Rover Centre in Huddersfield, and has been fitted with many parts from the later 90 models.

A second example of what the specialists can do is this fully rebuilt V8 Station Wagon. It now has full County specification — but County models were still two years away when this vehicle was originally built!

twin-carburettor type (from the 1973-1976 2200TC model), as this offers plenty of mid-range torque as well as a maximum of 115bhp.

Another common transplant in Land-Rovers is the Ford 3-litre V6 engine, which was used in that company's big saloon cars in the 1960s and 1970s. It gives around 145bhp, depending on version, and can be tuned for more power. Some companies have offered high-quality adaptor kits for the Land-Rover and unless you believe that a Land-Rover should have a Rover engine the Ford V6 can be a very good power unit for your Land-Rover.

With all these transplants, you should check that the associated modifications to the vehicle have been carried out to an acceptable standard. In some cases, it's necessary to cut the bulkhead to make room for the bigger engine, but not every home-modifier has made a decent job of rewelding!

Transmissions

The four-wheel-drive system of the Land-Rover limits the number of alternative gearboxes which can be used. Nevertheless, some rebuilders have replaced the rather agricultural gearbox of early models with the all-synchromesh Series III gearbox or even with later types. These later types, taken from Range Rovers and 90/110 Land-Rovers, bring with them permanent four-wheel drive. The early Range Rover four-speed gearbox with integral transfer box is probably the most common transplant. It is a rugged (and pretty agricultural) gearbox but has a tendency to consume its own oil and should be checked regularly. The five-speed Range Rover gearbox is much more user-friendly, and brings the added advantage of an overdrive fifth gear for motorway cruising. Remember, though, that not all five-speed gear-boxes are Range Rover boxes: some five-speed boxes fitted to Land-Rovers in the early 1980s were built in Spain to a different design and were rather less refined. Gearbox transplants such as these often entail propshaft modifications. Not every rebuilder has been aware of the need to balance modified propshafts in order to avoid vibration. A road-test will soon show up whether the job has been done thoroughly!

Customised Land-Rovers

The infinite adaptability of the Land-Rover also gives it an appeal to those who like their vehicles to be a very personal expression of themselves. Take an ex-military lightweight Land-Rover, add a Station Wagon body, a more powerful engine and some 'County' side stripes from a late Series III, and you have a vehicle which is still recognisably a Land-Rover but is very different from any which ever came off the production line at Solihull.

Many military lightweights were in fact professionally rebuilt in this way for sale during the 1980s. Other used Land-Rovers were also professionally reconditioned and rebuilt to incorporate items such as the County trim introduced in 1982. Such vehicles are very attractive purchases, but if you are looking at one, make sure the seller can prove that the conversion was carried out by one of the professionals rather than by a back-street garage.

What else might you find in a customised Land-Rover? Better seats are one thing — sometimes expensive Recaros but more often Rover P6 saloon seats or simply the de luxe versions of the standard offering. Side stripes might be the genuine factory article or any one of a number of aftermarket varieties. Let your own taste guide you here. Many people have also fitted bull bars (also known as 'roo bars). This accessory lends an aggressive air to the front of the vehicle but its value is questionable outside Australia (where fast-moving vehicles risk collision with kangaroos which wander about on the roads; the 'roo bar prevents damage to the lights and radiator if a collision occurs).

Lastly, many customised Land-Rovers wear neat eight-spoke wheels, and some have been fitted with wide wheels and tyres. Remember that wide wheels must not protrude beyond the bodywork (that's the law) and so wheelarch extensions will have to be fitted in almost every case. Usually, the 90/110 type are used, although there are special aftermarket types to suit the ex-military Lightweight. It's also worth remembering that wide wheels often make the steering unbearably heavy at parking speeds and can cause the ride to deteriorate noticeably. Whether you find that acceptable or not is up to you.

Competition vehicles

Many early short-wheelbase Land-Rovers have been modified for off-road competition use. Some have been so heavily modified that they are no longer legally usable on the road, and they are a subject all on their own. However, some off-road competition vehicles remain road-legal. Whether you like the image that comes with the roll-over bars, fire extinguishers, racing harness and other paraphernalia of an off-road racer is for you to decide. Just remember, though: like all Land-Rovers, these vehicles were built for a purpose, and that purpose was not comfortable on-road use. You have been warned!

Above: You can change things under the bonnet, too. This is a four-cylinder OHC Rover 2200 saloon engine installed in a Series III 88-inch Land-Rover. In fact, the conversion pictured was carried out by Rover's own Experimental Department, but many DIY owners have done similar jobs.

Left: If you want more power from your Land-Rover diesel engine, why not think about having a turbocharger fitted?

Above: The Perkins 4.182 3-litre engine has long been a favourite for Land-Rover diesel conversions. The benefits as compared to a four- or even a six-cylinder petrol engine are better performance, improved towing ability, and cheaper running costs. Professional conversions are not cheap, however.

Above, right: Also suitable as a conversion unit for Series III models is the VM six-cylinder turbodiesel. It gives superb performance and good fuel economy, but is again expensive to have fitted professionally.

Right: Off-road competition is now a thriving activity, and many Land-Rovers have been heavily modified to participate in it. Here is one such in action.

Above: If you like camping, perhaps a Carawagon conversion, with that company's famous elevating roof, would be a good buy…

Below: …and if you enjoy getting your vehicle wet and muddy, all Land-Rovers have remarkable rough-terrain ability (though the short-wheelbase models are best off-road). This is a Series III V8, doing what comes naturally.

6. Living with a Land-Rover

If you've already decided that a Land-Rover is what you want and that nothing else will do, then no amount of well-intentioned advice will make you change your mind. Not that a Land-Rover isn't a wise choice, of course; it's just that you do need to think quite carefully about what you're letting yourself (and family and friends) in for. This Chapter is designed to help you think the issues through.

The first issue to consider is *cost*. The purchase price of Land-Rovers varies widely, and the asking price isn't always dependent on condition. Station Wagons cost more than soft-tops; six-cylinders and V8s cost more than four-cylinders. Reconditioned vehicles also usually merit a higher price tag than 'original' vehicles of the same age. And because a Land-Rover is still essentially a working vehicle, a pristine low-mileage early model is going to attract only small numbers of interested buyers, none of whom will pay the inflated prices familiar in the classic car world.

None of the Land-Rovers covered in this book should be very expensive. A basket-case vehicle in need of a complete rebuild just to keep it on the road will sell for a couple of hundred pounds (if it sells at all). At the other end of the scale, a pristine V8 long-wheelbase Station Wagon will cost less than the cheapest two-year-old family hatchback.

While older Land-Rovers are generally cheap to purchase, they might not be so cheap to keep running. Fuel consumption of the six-cylinder and V8 long-wheelbase models can be alarmingly high (think in terms of under 15mpg, whatever the traffic conditions), while most of the four-cylinder petrol models struggle to reach 20mpg on a regular basis. Overdrive helps, but only if you do a lot of fast main-road or motorway driving, and you shouldn't in any case get much more than an extra 2mpg from an overdrive-equipped Land-Rover. If you want fuel economy, you need to go for one of the diesel-powered models. Even so, 25mpg would generally be a cause for celebration.

Repairs and maintenance, though, will be fairly inexpensive, unless you buy a real heap that needs constant attention. Land-Rovers are rugged and durable vehicles, designed to take a lot of punishment and to survive on minimal maintenance. That is not to say that you should ignore basic servicing requirements, of course: if you don't change the oil regularly, the engine will wear quickly, and if you don't change the plugs and air filter once in a while, performance will deteriorate. But a Land-Rover is nowhere near as sensitive to neglect as a more complex and highly-tuned vehicle. It might protest if you don't treat it properly, but it probably won't let you down completely.

It's also true to say that the working-vehicle image of a Land-Rover means that you won't be so sensitive to minor body damage as you would be with a car. Nothing looks more down-market than an expensive car with a large dent in the wing; but many Land-Rover owners would claim that a Land-Rover hasn't been properly broken-in until it's got a few battle scars on its bodywork. If someone dents the wing of your Land-Rover, you probably won't therefore feel the need to rush off to the nearest body shop and have it repaired. Land-Rover ownership induces a more relaxed attitude: leave the dent where it is or bash it out yourself.

Insurance? Not many people bother to go for fully-comprehensive insurance on a Land-Rover of this age: the vehicle's market-value simply doesn't justify the expense. Besides, it's pretty difficult to do so much damage to a Land-Rover that your insurers would want to write it off under a comprehensive policy. Your best bet is to go for Third Party, Fire and Theft cover. You'll probably be pleasantly surprised when you compare the premium with the premium asked for a family hatchback. Be careful, though, if you're dealing with a highly-modified vehicle. Tell your insurers exactly what's been done to it, and don't be surprised if they seem to be hesitant over insuring a 40-year-old vehicle with rather dodgy drum brakes into which you have transplanted an uprated V8 engine.

With many classic cars, the question of *storage* is critical. With a Land-Rover, it is one which rarely gets considered. The bodies are panelled in aluminium alloy and are designed to stand up to extremes of weather, so don't be too worried about leaving your Land-Rover parked outside. When did you last hear of anyone who put a Land-Rover away in a garage at night, anyway? Of course, if the soft top leaks in wet weather, that's a different matter...

Another issue which plagues classic-car owners is the inherent risk of leaving their pride and joy parked in the street overnight. What if someone comes along and runs a key across its shiny paint? What about the drunken driver who smashes into it and then disappears without a trace? And what if some joyrider decides to go for a spin?

As a Land-Rover owner, you probably won't have these worries. No-one wastes time scratching Land-Rover paint — it's usually too dull to show the marks, anyway. Any driver who runs into a parked Land-Rover is probably going to be unable to drive away afterwards. And, as for joyriders, they don't take Land-Rovers because they aren't fast enough.

Practicality also comes into the question of Land-Rover ownership. Whether a Land-Rover is practical enough for you depends very much on what you need from your means of transport. It's true that it was designed to be a practical vehicle, but remember that it was designed to be a practical *working* vehicle. It was thus intended to meet a quite different set of requirements from those associated with a saloon car.

If you do a lot of towing, a Land-Rover will be ideal. (This is especially so if it's a long-wheelbase model, as these offer greater stability). If you need a load-carrier, you could hardly do better than a long-wheelbase pick-up (especially a Series III or V8 HCPU). But if you carry passengers a lot, think carefully before you buy. Firstly, you will be disappointed with anything less than a Station Wagon. Even then, don't expect older members of the family to be enthusiastic about the levels of comfort. Similarly, think about the sort of driving you do. If a lot of it is long-distance work, you'll probably find the high noise levels in a Land-Rover a bit wearing.

Lastly, how *reliable* is a Land-Rover? Generally, by the vehicle's very nature, the answer is very reliable indeed. If treated decently, it will give years and years of trouble-free service, with none of the aforementioned risks and insecurities associated with a classic saloon or sports car. If mistreated, it will play up. Buy a good one, and it won't let you down. Buy a rough one, and you'll get exactly that.

A long-wheelbase Station Wagon makes an excellent people-carrier. The rearmost seats fold up out of the way and the bench seat folds forward to give an enormous load area, too. Comfort levels are not high, however. This is a Series III model; the County trim was plusher.

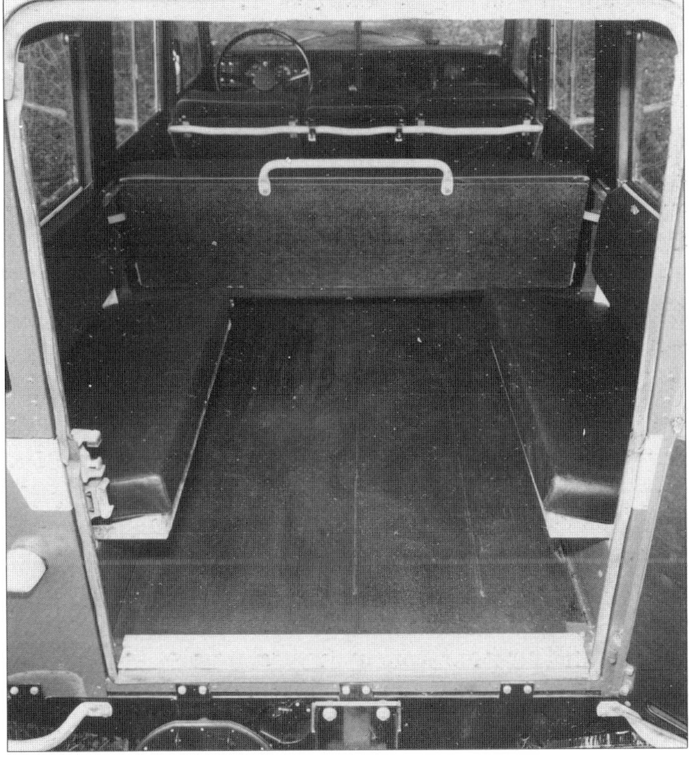

Left and below: Among other benefits, the ARC organises numerous events for its members. Pictured here is action from the 'Team Recovery' event at the 1989 ARC National Rally, held near Harrogate in Yorkshire. (Richard Thomas)

Opposite page: More action, this time from the 1990 'Competitive Safari'. (Richard Thomas)

7. Land-Rover support services

By comparison with the owners of some older vehicles, Land-Rover owners can count themselves extremely lucky. Not only does Land Rover Ltd through its Land Rover Parts subsidiary provide parts to keep older vehicles on the road, but so do literally hundreds of non-franchised specialists.

There is an important distinction to be drawn here, however. Land Rover Parts is primarily committed to the support of the current range of vehicles. It also caters extensively for Series III models, and even provides a full reconditioning service for these vehicles in some Third World countries. The wide interchangeability of parts between these and earlier vehicles means that Land Rover Parts can cater well for the Series II or Series IIA owner, as well. However, it is important to remember that the company's aim is to keep vehicles running, and not to provide a parts service for the relatively small number of restorers who wish to maintain their vehicles in original condition. Thus, if a Series III or later part will fit an early vehicle, that will be the one available when stocks of the earlier type run out.

This position is one which suits the majority of Land-Rover owners. As we have seen elsewhere, most Land-Rovers have been modified to some extent and, as most of them work for a living, owners are content with supplies of parts which simply keep their vehicles on the road. For those other owners who are keen to keep their vehicles in 'original' condition, the only solution in many cases is to deal with one of the non-franchised specialists. These companies are small enough to cope with the relatively low sales volume of parts peculiar to Series I or early Series II vehicles. Some even arrange for limited batch remanufacture of unobtainable parts from time to time: examples have been front bulkheads and canvas tilt covers for early 80-inch models.

There are Land Rover Parts outlets at all the Land-Rover dealerships. Genuine parts are also available through many of the non-franchised specialists, and these specialists also offer non-genuine or reproduction parts, which are often considerably cheaper than the 'factory' equivalents. They also offer a considerable range of accessory items which are not and never have been available from Land Rover. Such items do not, of course, carry a Land Rover warranty, and some can invalidate Land Rover guarantees.

Left: Ready for inspection. Concours line-up at the 1990 ARC National Rally. (Richard Thomas)

Below: Flying the flag. The Series II Club stand at the 1992 National Rally. (Richard Thomas)

Land-Rover Clubs

There are also plenty of Land-Rover clubs for the enthusiast to join. The governing organisation to which most of these are affiliated is the **Association of Rover Clubs.** A full list of all the clubs would take up more room than is available here, and would in any case probably become out of date very quickly because contact addresses do change with the appointment of new club officials. Suffice it to say that the ARC-affiliated clubs include many regional ones, that several of these cater for off-road competition and camping/caravanning interests, and that several other clubs cater for those whose interest lies primarily in the historical and restoration side of Land Rovers. The latter include the **Land-Rover Register (1948-1951)**, the **Land-Rover Series One Club**, and the **Land-Rover Series Two Club**. For a current list of clubs and contact addresses, you should write to the **ARC, c/o Andrew Stavordale, 65 Longmead Avenue, Hazel Grove, Stockport, Cheshire SK7 5PJ**.

Those whose interest is primarily in off-road activities might also like to think about joining the **All Wheel Drive Club** which, as its name suggests, caters for all types of off-road vehicles and not just for Land-Rovers. The AWDC maintains a very full calendar of events and can be contacted at **P.O. Box 6, Fleet, Hampshire GU13 9QL**.

Reading matter. An abundance of books and magazines provides enthusiasts with the means to further their knowledge and enjoyment of Land-Rovers.

Further Land-Rover Reading

If you enjoy reading about Land-Rovers — and can find the time to do so — you will find plenty of material to choose from. The regular monthly magazines carry advertising from all the leading non-franchised specialists and are particularly valuable in this respect. The only magazine devoted exclusively to Land Rover products is the monthly (and very well-informed) **Land Rover Owner**, although there are several others which cover wider off-roading and 4x4 interests. In Britain, these include **Off Road and Four-Wheel Drive**, **International Off-Roader**, and **4x4**.

There have also been several books written about Land-Rovers. A few are out of print, but might still be found secondhand at autojumbles or in specialist shops. Two books by Graham Robson, **The Land-Rover** and **The Range Rover/Land-Rover** (published by David & Charles), are reliable introductions to the subject, and Ken and Julie Slavin's **Land-Rover, the Unbeatable 4x4** (Haynes Publishing) is a good general history with an interesting chapter on the company's Special Projects Department, written by its former head, George Mackie.

A model-by-model survey will be found in the present author's **The Land-Rover 1948-1988** (Motor Racing Publications), while **Land-Rover, The Early Years** (written and published by Tony Hutchings) tells the story of the pre-production vehicles in painstaking detail.

A wide-ranging photo-and-caption history is provided by **Classics In Colour: Land Rover** (Windrow & Greene), again by the present author. Also well illustrated in colour is Chris Bennett's **Land-Rover** (Osprey Publishing).

There is a partial history of British military Land-Rovers in Les Geary's **The Fighting Rovers** (Ian Henry), and a colourful look at a more recent conflict in Bob Morrison's **British Land Rovers In The Gulf** (LRO books).

A useful guide to all things Land-Rover is the **Land-Rover Directory**, last published in 1987 but due to appear in a new edition.

Mack's Land-Rover Directory '93. (McGuigan Motorsport) is a comprehensive listing of after-market services.

Detailed 'hands-on' advice is furnished in **Land-Rover Series I, II & III: Guide To Purchase & DIY Restoration** by Lindsay Porter (Haynes Publishing); in the maintenance guide, **Know Your Land-Rover**, by Robert Ivins (LRO Books); and in **Land-Rover Restoration Tips & Techniques**, which is published by Brooklands Books in conjunction with Land Rover Owner magazine and contains much reliable guidance. Perhaps the most useful practical books of all, though, are the many **factory manuals, parts catalogues and handbooks** which have been reissued in their entirety by Brooklands Books. A complete list of these, along with details of the several collected **Land-Rover road tests** they have published, can be obtained by phoning Brooklands on 0932 865051.